David Calogero Centorbi

THE ELOQUENCE OF DEPARTURE

SurVision Books

First published in 2024 by
SurVision Books
Dublin, Ireland
Reggio di Calabria, Italy
www.survisionmagazine.com

Copyright © David Calogero Centorbi, 2024

Cover image: "Things to Come" by Victoria Chernyakhivska
© Victoria Chernyakhivska, 2024

Design © SurVision Books, 2024

ISBN: 978-1-912963-49-2

This book is in copyright. No part of this publication may be reproduced, stored in a retrieval system, or transmitted in any form or by any means without the prior permission in writing from the publisher.

Acknowledgments

Grateful acknowledgment is made to the editors of the following, in which some of these poems, or versions of them, originally appeared:

Horror, Sleaze, Trash: "I Saw the Sweaty Scales"

Live Nude Poems: "Barbed Laughter"

Outcast Press: "Apologies Folded Up Along with a Broken Memory"

Punk Noir Magazine: "Progression with Sharps and Flats"

SurVision Magazine: "The Space Between Your Sighs" and "The Cracks of Knowing"

There Is a Pale Aching: "A Thin Slice of Anxiety"

CONTENTS

Preface	5
The Space Between Your Sighs	6
The Cracks of Knowing	7
The Light Left Dancing	8
When the Prayers Broke Over You	10
There Is Hissing	13
A Voice That Cannot Offer	14
Progression with Sharps and Flats	15
The Cloves of Want	21
Apologies Folded Up Along with a Broken Memory	22
Barbed Laughter	24
I Saw the Sweaty Scales	27
There Is a Pale Aching	28

Preface

All your promises
like a diamond rain
fall

cutting
whispers of blood
into our

once upon a time
laughter.

The Space Between Your Sighs

The space between your sighs
scared me the most. In that stillness, I knew
you hid fingernails and chalkboards.

I knew I couldn't outrun
the sound of that stillness,

and I knew I couldn't stay—
all I had were hands that wouldn't clench.

So I held up the barrel of a dream:

its open eyes wept pardons,
its open mouth spoke forgetting.

I said, *Can you see yourself here?*

And you took my question,

folded it into a porcelain nightingale,
threw it into the air,

and asked me to watch it
try to fly.

The Cracks of Knowing

The cracks of knowing
on the crying
marble that folded its

eye-filled fingers around
the wet hunger
I felt when I tried to embrace

the tilted prayers
you breathed
out into the darkness—

such flames, such embers
pirouetting into the mouth
of the fragrant black sky—

given back to you as silken,
cold laughter.

The Light Left Dancing

1.

Darkness repeats its touch,
remembered: forehead, cheek, shoulders

bowed
you speak to each ray of grass,
each tear:

shattered bottle:
voice broken, the color of barley.

2.

Embrace: a hole
dug into the sand,
your steps repeat, imprints
collapse.

Songs through the weeds
hush
louder than morning.

3.

So many waves:
faces shunned,
your body flows with the taste of winter.

Each stone rehearses—

the circle in the sand still bleeds.

4.

Your fingers open—
blossoms scattered over the water.

Your lungs hold forever
the changing seasons.

When the Prayers Broke Over You

1.

When the prayers
broke over you,
and would lose
their potency
to speak or dance,

you would settle for fondling
because you always had to find
the cheapest way out
of forgetting
of giving,
even hands cupped with water.

2.

The shards of wind that flicked
the hair off your forehead
had enough of your voice—a sound
that never knew the words, serenade
or settling; a sound,
like a dropped
bag of nails

aching the veins of even the smallest
ray of moonlight.

3.

The proper place for blood
is at the end of a kiss

was the mantra you
whispered into any ear that lay
next to you—pleasant as they may have been

you only saw bones, like they were candles

something to illuminate your cracked
affection grown over with
a sick moss you created
from the sticky truths you
would hang up

over the shower curtain rod

then watch their
last dusty breaths
fall to the floor.

There Is Hissing

There is hissing
from the wine glasses
melting
down
your lipstick
stains, setting the pillows
on fire:

hairs of loss scattering into the air,
specks of lies littering the walls,
smoke filled with tongues
confused and asking,

Who is the savior of crying sand,
of crippled roses?

And where is the table you
tore from the yes I gave you?

...set now with the severed
heads of remembering.

A Voice That Cannot Offer

Your broken words
scattered like cigarette butts
along the highway.
The pain of your caress
is shattered glass
laughter
that hits and drips
down from the ceiling over
your turnstile bed.

Those are not tearful memories,

they are the cracked
bleeding pictures you left
of yourself

that I swept up
lifted the trash
bin lid
and threw out,

finally hearing
the song of your goodbye.

Progression with Sharps and Flats

1.

the candle
and spoon,
the bubble—

the still-born lie
hanging
you
breath by breath.

2.

sad glass
and that dead rainbow through it

the sun cast on the wall
when I found your needle;

I thought your belt
was a snake.

you always had to have a pet.

sometimes a rodent.
sometimes a bowl fish,

but always something

for you to let die.

3.

The trickle of blood running down your arm:
the pinprick hole:
the black and blue stain:
the never filled:
the always needing—

your only words
I knew were true.

4.

you screamed
out your
detox
gibberish—

the sharp hurt that couldn't be dulled

by everything of me

I tried to give you.

5.

the haze of hours,

voiceless rot,
no touch, no touch,

just cracking,
and your sweat that never dried.

6.

you burned yourself away,

but I didn't turn you
into the ashes

you always believed
you were.

The Cloves of Want

The cloves of want
light up
your lies
you break
open
on the
cutting board, a torte
of perturbed
tears

this time

thrown through
the bedroom
window

at our
hanging façades,
wet with moldy,
lost years.

Apologies Folded Up Along with a Broken Memory

Sometimes there was a song that pierced your tongue.
Sometimes I became the forgery you said I was, so
even the shards of wonder had meaning:

a shattered bottle against a sweaty bible.
A salty sunset.
The time I fell,
turned inside out with pleasure,
into your questions...

And oh, there were prayers:
such a slick confusion because your smile
smelled like a late-night shot.
I tried to taste the flames.
I tried to see your face unfiltered, to smell the blood
of all those tapped hearts
wet with anonymous desire,

but there was always
only the ceiling
and its cracked
cold laughter,

as I closed my eyes,

as I tried to breathe,

as I tried to call out your name.

Barbed Laughter

1.

Barbed laughter from a night
of bitter parades:

the holy left hanging held in no palms,
genuflections to thorned spittled hearts.

You heard the tears
as they rolled
down my cheek,
jaundiced and frantic.

2.

In what nightmare will you sleep in next
turning children's eyes into cringing stones,
their tongues into lonely red carpets?

I asked you to pour your pleadings on the wind
and scatter their rusty tears up to the sun—
light of future cold
and will-less destruction.

3.

You stood over
the stillpain on the altar—cries long lost,
forgotten curled fingers—
and caressed the smiles of lies,
stroked the silky manes of illusion.
There was a fire there
that had never breathed or eaten.
Its orange lips cracked, the valleys
holding pails of dizzy, dying lovers.

And you kept singing:

Until the end of time,
Blood, forgiveness, and laughter
Will be mine.

I Saw the Sweaty Scales

I saw the sweaty scales
And their cracked notes
sliding down
into a now
stillborn melody.

A melody, that once, when our legs and feet
could breathe, we held one another and whispered
stars and thunder into each other's ears,
our passion melting the jealous mirrors, until

the sharp tears started spreading across the floor
pushing us toward shot glasses filled with bitter-blood-light—

a drink we would soon raise
to our once imagined, endless horizons.

There Is a Pale Aching

1.

Your blushes asked me
once for lies.
The asking withered off the tongue.

Sometimes, there were sirens.
Sometimes, silence etching

broken hearts on bedroom windows.

2.

You saw grace in cracked
bouquets. Felt forgiveness
on cold fingers.

In the bedroom,
candles dripped a sordid wax—

your short hard breaths. Your silhouette
crying to dizzy, satin sheets.

3.

I offered you
the places you tried to forget,

the confessions
turned to blue stone,

the sweet taste of moonlight
cupped with unintentional supplication,

but you just smiled
and whispered:

Harm smells like freshly
cut grass, its deep brown eyes
tease like bourbon,

and there are only so many prayers
the frigid black sky can hold

until it finally drowns you
in its merciful rain.

Selected Poetry Titles Published by SurVision Books

Contemporary Tangential Surrealist Poetry: An Anthology
Edited by Tony Kitt
ISBN 978-1-912963-44-7

Invasion: An Anthology of Ukrainian Poetry about the War
Edited by Tony Kitt
ISBN 978-1-912963-32-4

Noelle Kocot. *Humanity*
(New Poetics: USA)
ISBN 978-1-9995903-0-7

Marc Vincenz. *Einstein Fledermaus*
(New Poetics: USA)
ISBN 978-1-912963-20-1

Helen Ivory. *Maps of the Abandoned City*
(New Poetics: England)
ISBN 978-1-912963-04-1

Tony Kitt. *The Magic Phlute*
(New Poetics: Ireland)
ISBN 978-1-912963-08-9

Clayre Benzadón. *Liminal Zenith*
(New Poetics: USA)
ISBN 978-1-912963-11-9

Thomas Townsley. *Tangent of Ardency*
(New Poetics: USA)
ISBN 978-1-912963-15-7

Mikko Harvey & Jake Bauer. *Idaho Falls*
(Winner of James Tate Poetry Prize 2018)
ISBN 978-1-912963-02-7

John Bradley. *Spontaneous Mummification*
(Winner of James Tate Poetry Prize 2019)
ISBN 978-1-912963-13-3

Charles Kell. *Pierre Mask*
(Winner of James Tate Poetry Prize 2019)
ISBN 978-1-912963-19-5

Charles Borkhuis. *Spontaneous Combustion*
(Winner of James Tate Poetry Prize 2021)
ISBN 978-1-912963-30-0

Noah Falck and Matt McBride. *Prerecorded Weather*
(Winner of James Tate Poetry Prize 2022)
ISBN 978-1-912963-39-3

Michael Zeferino Spring. *Kahlo's Window*
(Winner of James Tate Poetry Prize 2022)
ISBN 978-1-912963-40-9

Jeffrey Cyphers Wright. *Fuel for Love*
(Winner of James Tate Poetry Prize 2023)
ISBN 978-1-912963-45-4

George Kalamaras. *That Moment of Wept*
ISBN 978-1-9995903-7-6

George Kalamaras. *Through the Silk-Heavy Rains*
ISBN 978-1-912963-28-7

Order our books from http://survisionmagazine.com

www.ingramcontent.com/pod-product-compliance
Lightning Source LLC
Chambersburg PA
CBHW061315040426
42444CB00010B/2654